Tell It Slant

STUDY GUIDE

Tell It Slant

STUDY GUIDE

Eugene H. Peterson & Peter Santucci

WILLIAM B. EERDMANS PUBLISHING COMPANY
GRAND RAPIDS, MICHIGAN / CAMBRIDGE, U.K.

Published 2008 by
Wm. B. Eerdmans Publishing Co.
2140 Oak Industrial Drive N.E., Grand Rapids, Michigan 49505 /
P.O. Box 163, Cambridge CB3 9PU U.K.
www.eerdmans.com

Library of Congress Cataloging-in-Publication Data

Peterson, Eugene H., 1932-
Tell it slant study guide / Eugene H. Peterson and Peter Santucci.
p.   cm.
ISBN 978-0-8028-6379-9 (pbk.: alk. paper)
1. Jesus Christ — Parables — Textbooks.
2. Jesus Christ — Prayers — Textbooks.
3. Bible. N.T. Gospels — Language, style — Textbooks.
I. Santucci, Peter.   II. Title.

BT375.3.P472   2008
226'.06 — dc22

200839100

Tell It Slant is published in association with the literary agency of Alive Communications, Inc., 7680 Goddard Street, Suite 200, Colorado Springs, CO 80920

Contents

Contents

PART II
Jesus in His Prayers

Contents

Preface

How is the Christian life shaped in us? How do we become attuned to Jesus and his way — or "The Way" as the first Christians referred to the Jesus movement?

It's a question I've always been interested in as a follower of Jesus. From my earliest days as a kid who went to Sunday school, I've had this sense that being a Christian actually means something and that something has less to do with dressing up and showing up for church services than with who I am and how I go about living in this world.

But what is it exactly? And how do I get it into me?

The question didn't go away as I became a youth group leader and then a small group Bible study leader and then a pastor. In fact, the question only intensified, for I was no longer dealing with how the Christian life is shaped in me individually, but I was now responsible for others. How is Christ formed in them?

There are all sorts of programs and books and videos promising the secrets of discipleship. But instead of describing discipleship as the art of following Jesus, they presented it more like a science. Everything was clearly laid out: read and memorize Scripture, pray, go to church, evangelize, go to youth group or Bible study or prayer meeting or potlucks or whatever.

But following Jesus is more of an art than a science. And there's something about how we use language, the ways we speak and write, that turns the same words that speak words of worship, prayer, truth, love, and down-to-earth living into words that blaspheme, curse, lie, gossip, and bully. The same language, holy and exalted by the One who spoke creation into being, is easily abused even by those who follow the Word.

This makes our goal of having Christ formed in us that much more difficult, because the main tool we have is words, language spoken, written, prayed, preached, sung.

Eugene Peterson sees the Christian life — the life of Christ — shaped in us by a recovery of language through an immersion in the way Jesus himself used language. And though Jesus spoke in other forms of language as well, Peterson immerses us in the stories Jesus told and the prayers he prayed. These two forms of language — story and prayer — when engaged in the Jesus way, bring with them the Jesus life.

You can use the tool of this study guide on your own and gain from it, but it is best used in a community of Christians. There's a certain level of honesty that can be reached only when questions are answered aloud in front of people who know us, and honest speech becomes a truth event in which we articulate things that we may not have intended to say but that change us as a result. Silent thoughts that don't escape the mind rarely do that.

This study guide is formatted for a twenty-session study, with each chapter receiving its own attention. Each session has a summary of the section covered. I've included this for the sake of the group leader(s). You may or may not want to read this aloud before the group discussion. One problem with reading summaries aloud in small groups is that such summaries can lead to laziness, as when I was in eighth grade and read CliffNotes on *Moby Dick* instead of the complete novel.

Along with questions for interaction, I've included quotations to consider. Eugene Peterson is eminently quotable, and I've had to restrain myself with the number of quotations included. (My wife was helpful in that process.) At times we need questions to spark our interaction, but at other times, simply reading a powerful and representative quotation is even more effective in generating interaction.

But remember, this guide includes a lot of quotations and questions. Make sure you consider the amount of time you have available for conversation and discussion before you pick which ones to use. Simply starting with the first quotation or the first question and trying to get through them all would be a mistake, unless you are using this guide for personal study. No group I know could have any depth of interaction while dealing with all the quotations and questions.

I've also ended each session with a prayer. I've called these sections either "Praying along the Road to Samaria" or "Praying with Jesus."

If you're using this study guide with a group that has been meeting together for a while, you probably have an established rhythm and way of interacting. If you're fairly new at this or are willing to explore a different shape for your time together, here is how our community groups operate (the groups I had in mind when I wrote this guide). It's fairly simple. We gather for a meal. The sharing of food makes it much easier to share our lives. Church-related talk is not permitted during meals. Talk about anything and everything else is encouraged. After the meal, we have our discussion time. Next, we take a break for dessert. And then we gather again for prayer. That's all. It's not a fool-proof technique, but it's a basic rhythm that makes sure not only that we are discussing the passage or book for that evening but also that we're engaging each other as friends and praying for each other.

Just as Jesus' stories were told in the company of his disciples, this study guide was written in the company of faithful Jesus followers, even if they were not always aware of the project. My wife Charlene is my main conversation partner. My covenant group told stories and prayed with me, as did my new companions on the way: the Tuesday Dads and Chad Hanson. Coffee and work table provided by Rock the Caffe.

Ordinary Time 2008   PETER SANTUCCI

PART I

Jesus in His Stories

Jesus in Samaria: Luke 9:51–19:27

(pp. 1-5 and 9-31)

Theme

Using language to open up and relate instead of to hide and control.

Summary

God (and the rest of us, too) reveals himself in words, in language. And even though Jesus never wrote a word that has been preserved, he spoke. It's this spoken, oral nature of his ministry that draws us into the conversations where many of these words were spoken.

The first speaking we generally think of with Jesus is preaching. This proclamation of the good news engages us directly. And it does so by reshaping our imaginations.

Jesus was also a teacher, using words to bring together the parts of our lives. Teaching helps us develop an intelligent and faithful obedience in all the areas of our lives.

Preaching and teaching are essential, keeping us aware of God and wary of the not-God idolatries that surround us. But beyond this formal speaking is the informal speaking of small talk, which makes up most of our speaking. While Mark shows Jesus preaching and Matthew shows Jesus teaching, Luke shows him engaging in the informal speech of daily life. We see this especially in the center of Luke's Gospel (9:51–19:27) in the stories Jesus tells while on the road. It is the very ordinariness of these stories that connects the kingdom of God to the day-to-day lives of Jesus' disciples. Instead of using urgent, crisis words in the face of his imminent crucifixion, he uses the language of the everyday to prepare for post-resurrection, everyday living.

Most of life takes place "in between," on the road, in parentheses. We spend little of our lives reading our Bibles, listening to sermons, in the company of our small groups and worshiping communities. We need a faith for the in between, for dealing with people and conditions and even ourselves in the otherwise parenthetical parts of our lives. There is a place for memorization (bringing Scripture and preaching/teaching into daily life) and for improvisation. Jesus' stories teach us to improvise within the context of Scripture.

The name for Jesus' improvised stories that teach us to improvise on what he has preached and taught elsewhere is parable. Parables aren't new material. Rather, they point us to what we've missed or dismissed. Their non-religious, storied nature disarms our resistance to them and involves us in them at the same time.

There are many people ("Samaritans") who have a deep aversion to God-language and have defended themselves against it. Jesus' parables skirt these defenses, telling the gospel "slant."

The intensity of what Jesus is calling for necessitates parable. Its urgency actually reduces attentiveness if it is told too straightforwardly. The closer he gets to the end of his life and the hotter the heat gets, the less direct Jesus becomes.

All language is holy and has the potential of being Spirit-uttered. The Holy Spirit is no less present and active and speaking when we are "on the road" than when we are in the sanctuary. Just because we do not mention God or are even aware of his presence doesn't mean that the Spirit isn't inspiring or accompanying what we or others are speaking. Often we recognize God's voice in retrospect.

Spiritual direction is the name Christians have been using for ages to describe the conversational practice of paying attention to the formation of persons in Christ. This important practice helps work out the general truth proclaimed in preaching and teaching in Spirit-guided personal interactions, moving us from the general to the particular. Unlike programs that lump people into categories, these one-on-one conversations deal with particularities. While in spiritual direction it is important to pay attention to all of a person's life — "to the words we are using when we don't think we are saying anything of significance" (p. 26) — a spiritual director pays special attention to a person's praying.

And though trained spiritual directors have an important role in the Christian community, anyone can learn to listen for God in the lives of other Jesus followers, engaging in spontaneous, unpremeditated conversations that are nonetheless Spirit-conversations.

It is tempting to take the bulldozer, Zebedee-brother approach to any lack of faith that we come up against instead of listening for the voice of God in the midst of it. The parables of Jesus on the road through Samaria are just such a listening to God's voice in an inhospitable land.

Definition

"Spiritual direction is one person intentionally and prayerfully immersing himself or herself in the casual ordinary life of any ordinary Christian." (p. 25)

Quotes for Consideration

"Preaching is language that involves us personally with God's action in the present." (p. 11)

"[Jesus] wasn't so much handing out information as reshaping our imaginations with metaphors so that we could take in the living multidimensioned truth that is Jesus." (p. 12)

"We often dichotomize our lives into public and private, spiritual and secular, cut up our lives into separate parts, and stuff the parts into labeled cubbyholes for convenient access when we feel like dealing with them." (p. 12)

"Inconspicuously, even surreptitiously, a parable *involves* the hearer." (p. 19)

"A parable is not ordinarily used to tell us something new but to get us to notice something that we have overlooked although it has been right there before us for years. Or it is used to get us to take seriously something we have dismissed as unimportant because we have never seen the point of it." (p. 19)

"When the words of Jesus become the stuff of arguments, verbal tools for

manipulation, attempts at control, the life drains out of them and
there they are, a raked-up pile of dead leaves on the ground." (p. 22)

"The Holy Spirit is as present in our spontaneous and casual conversations as in formal preaching and teaching." (p. 22)

"A great deal of Spirit-inspired, or Spirit-accompanied, language takes
place when we do not know it, whether it comes from our own
mouths or the mouths of others." (p. 23)

"The fact is that almost all words are holy and God speaks to and through
us by the very nature of language itself." (p. 24)

"General directions, useful as they are, don't take into account the details
that face us as holiness takes root in the particular social and personal place we are planted." (p. 25)

"Especially, we need personal attention given to our prayers, for prayer is
the practice by which all that we are, all that we believe and do, is
transformed into the action of the Spirit working his will in the details of our dailiness." (p. 25)

"Prayer consists in the transformation of what we do in the name of Jesus
to what the Holy Spirit does in us as we follow Jesus." (p. 25)

"Any Christian can, and many Christians do, *listen* and help us *listen* to the
undercurrents of our language, the unspoken and unheard, the silences that undergird so much of the language that we use unthink-
ingly." (p. 26)

Questions for Interaction

Do you use words more to reveal your "vast interior," to give information, or to get people to do things? What percent of the words you
use each day go to each?

Why does Luke slow down his Gospel to listen to Jesus telling stories?

What difficulties do you face in following Jesus during the "in between"
areas of your life? What relationships or circumstances are the most
difficult? And what makes them so?

How much of what you've experienced this week related directly to last
Sunday's sermon? How might on-the-road conversations and stories fill in the gaps?

Parables tell us about God without talking directly about God. What movies, novels, musicians, artists, etc. have done this for you? Share examples.

How well do you respond when someone tells you to change something in your life? How well do you respond when you hear or see a story that leads you to the same conclusion?

Who are you in conversation with during the week who might be resistant to God-talk? How might parable-like conversations enable you to talk about God without actually talking about God with them?

What do you find more persuasive — a well-reasoned argument or an engaging story? Why?

Have you ever had a conversation that you didn't realize was about God until later?

Is it possible to listen for God when we're not thinking about God? How so?

Praying along the Road to Samaria

Lord, you use your Word so well to reveal yourself. But I find myself using words to hide, conceal, misdirect, deceive, tear down, and make things abstract. I am a person of unclean lips. Teach me a new way of using words so that I may be more like you, who spoke and new life came into being. Through Jesus the Word. Amen.

SESSION 2

The Neighbor: Luke 10:25-37

(pp. 32-43)

Theme

Stopping the godtalk and getting on with loving our neighbors.

Summary

Opposition and hostility are no surprise to those who follow the Jesus way. When the heat gets turned up, we can either drop out or exuberantly dive into this discipleship.

A lawyer (that is, biblical scholar) takes on Jesus, and for good reason: a fraudulent Messiah is deadly. As a good lawyer, he asks for advice ("What must I do to inherit eternal life?") instead of interrogating Jesus. After he honors Jesus with a question, Jesus honors him back with a question of his own, and a relational conversation has begun. Instead of a debate about objective information, a dialog with personal interaction is under way. And quickly, the tester becomes the one being tested.

Instead of the vulnerability of relationship with God and others, the scholar, like us, seeks the control of self-justification — looking right without being righteous. But Jesus uncovers this power play through the telling of the Good Samaritan parable. The scholar had asked for a definition of the word "neighbor," but instead of a definition Jesus creates a neighbor, moving from ideas to relationships. Jesus stops the godtalk by his story and sends the scholar (and us) to be a neighbor, living love instead of talking about it. Abstract faith becomes lived love.

Quotes for Consideration

"Following Jesus isn't something we put off until we have first done what we want to do." (p. 32)

"Following Jesus doesn't take place on our terms. We follow Jesus on his terms." (p. 32)

"There is danger that we will become overly excited at what we see going on around us and neglect the center, our heaven-inscribed identities, out of which the work develops. Not what we do, but who we are 'in heaven' anchors the joy." (p. 34)

"Self-justification is a verbal device for restoring the appearance of rightness without doing anything about the substance." (p. 39)

"A person can hide undetected for a long time, maybe even for a lifetime, behind religious questions." (p. 40)

"Jesus' story puts a full stop for all time to all the variations on the question, 'Who is my neighbor?' From that time and right down to the present, the question is, 'Will I be a neighbor?' As Heinrich Greeven puts it, 'One cannot define one's neighbor; one can only be a neighbor.'" (p. 42)

"Love is not a subject to be discussed. . . . [I]t is as a verb that it springs into life." (p. 43)

"No more questions. No more answers. No more godtalk. Go and love." (p. 43)

Questions for Interaction

How might a Bible study *about* Scripture keep us from actually engaging *with* Scripture? How might it keep us from needing to obey God in Scripture?

How good of a listener are you? How good a questioner?

Who do you know who asks really good questions? What is their "trick"?

Who is your neighbor? How will you go beyond your difficulties in being a neighbor?

What imperatives (like "love your neighbor") have you left as ideas instead of obediently participated in?

What other stories outside of the ones in Scripture have shown you what it means to love your neighbor?

Who in particular is Jesus calling you to love right now?

Which group of people do you know by their ethnicity, religion, lifestyle, affiliation, etc., rather than as a neighbor? What would it look like to "re-neighbor" them?

Praying along the Road to Samaria

Lord of love, I've spent far too much time talking about love and not enough time loving my difficult and different neighbors. Open my eyes to my neighbors and get me moving, by your Spirit, to love them. In Jesus, whose cross teaches me love each day. Amen.

The Friend: Luke 11:1-13

(pp. 44-55)

Theme

Getting personal, relational, down-to-earth to avoid the devil's tool of abstraction.

Summary

Abstraction kills life. Whenever we move from the personal to the general, death results.

God is not an idea, a cause, or a feeling. God is a Person, revealed primarily in Jesus. But we reduce and generalize God easily. One place we see this is in our praying. Formality in prayer kills God's "humanity" — we speak to an It, not a Person. Instead of prayers from the gut, we fall into pious clichés. It's no surprise then that the disciples' one request to be taught had to do with prayer.

Jesus' response is surprising: a thirty-eight-word prayer. But praying is not helped by techniques or information. What the disciples wanted was a relationship with God like the one they saw in Jesus.

By pairing this prayer, addressed to "Father," with a parable addressed to "Friend," Jesus emphasizes the emphatically relational nature of prayer. Not a formula built from general principles, prayer is emphatically personal and particular — personal address that expects a personal response. And by using imperatives, the prayer and parable suggest that praying changes things, actively engaging God and reaching into the future to bring something new to pass. Things in the parable don't go smoothly, but they are resolutely personal — friend, friend, friend.

Requests for bread are central to both the prayer and the parable, tying both to the physical and the immediate, not to spiritual-seeming ideas, and opening our eyes to God's presence and actions in the details of our lives.

"Bread" also emphasizes our basic neediness. We don't pray out of wealth, but out of poverty. God has what we need. To be truly human is to be truly needy, poor, empty, impoverished, not self-sufficient. In other words, true humans are completely dependent on the Father of Jesus and ready for the actions of the Spirit.

Quotes for Consideration

"When any part of life is abstracted from the particular, formulated into a generalization, bureaucratized into a project, reduced to a cause, life itself is killed, or at least diminished considerably." (p. 44)

"When we deal with God, we are not dealing with a spiritual principle, a religious idea, an ethical cause, or a mystical feeling. We are dealing personally with Jesus, who is dealing personally with us." (p. 44)

"Prayer may well be the single aspect of our language most in danger of losing touch with the sheer grittiness of our humanity. We lose touch with our humanity when we deprive God of his humanity." (p. 46)

"Somehow [the disciples] have come to the realization that following him does not mean imitating what he does or repeating what he says. It means cultivating a relation with God the way they observe Jesus doing it." (p. 48)

"Frequenting a place of worship is a good way to learn to pray; attending a workshop on prayer is not. Associating with a person who you know prays is a good way to learn to pray (whether you talk about prayer or not); reading another book on prayer is not." (p. 49)

"Prayer can be learned only in the vocabulary and grammar of personal relationship: Father! Friend! It can never be a matter of getting the right words in the right order." (p. 51)

"When God became human in Jesus, he showed us how to become complete human beings before him. We do it the way Jesus did it, by becoming absolutely needy and dependent on the Father. Only when we stand emptied, stand impoverished before God can we receive what only empty hands can receive." (p. 54)

"We do not become less needy, less dependent when we pray; we become more needy, more dependent — which is to say, more human." (p. 55)

"Holy Spirit is God's way of being personally with us in all our listening and speaking and acting. God in all particulars of our lives and our friends' and neighbors' lives. God comprehensively and personally present." (p. 55)

Questions for Interaction

In what ways have you depersonalized God by thinking of him as an idea, force, or dogma?

What clichés do you repeat in your prayers? What do they say about your relationship with God?

When are your prayers most from the gut, most honest, most personal?

Why did the disciples ask Jesus to teach them to pray when they had the Psalms as a rich prayer book? How is the prayer Jesus taught similar to the Psalms? How are they different?

Why is it important that the one thing the disciples ask to learn from Jesus doesn't have to do with behavior, but with prayer, with how to relate with his Father?

Do you believe that it is possible to get in on the same relationship with God that Jesus had with his Father? What keeps you from experiencing that now?

What would it be like to pray like Jesus? How much guilt would there be? How much joy? How much (mutual) respect?

Have you ever heard someone "preach" in their praying (or done so yourself)? How does this ruin our praying?

How personal is the language of your praying? Even if you consider your praying to be personal, what keeps it from being more so?

How do formulas for prayer, as popular as they may be, endanger the relational nature of our praying?

Do you have a tendency to pray for "spiritual" things and not for basic physical things — gas for your car, food for your table, clothing for your body? How does praying for mundane things like bread change our relationship with God?

In what areas of life do you have expertise or competence? How do your abilities retard your praying in these areas? How can you restore a poverty perspective that will enrich your praying?

Praying along the Road to Samaria

Yahweh, our covenant-making God, you know us each by name. In your book, no one is a personality type, political demographic, or ethnic subgroup. You are absolutely personal in all your dealings with us. But we reduce people to traits and lump them into groups, and we even turn you into an abstract idea. Take away from us our tendency toward abstraction and ground us in real relationships, with you — Father, Son, and Holy Spirit — and with those you have surrounded us with. In the name of Jesus. Amen.

SESSION 4

The Barn Builder: Luke 12:13-21

(pp. 56-64)

Theme

Poverty and neediness before God in a covetous, self-sufficient world.

Summary

A man asks Jesus to mediate in a legal dispute, something rabbis were often asked to do. But Jesus refuses, discerning the sin of covetousness beneath the call for justice. The man's technique is textbook: use something everyone agrees as good as a disguise for sin. It's a technique used by religious people the world over. In fact, our greatest temptations follow suit, sins disguised as good things.

Parables are neither illustrations nor explanations that can be understood by observation. They are doors, drawing spectators into becoming participants. We are free to enter them or not, because the way God changes us is through invitation, not invasion. His truth doesn't come as a stick, but as a story.

Greed is a symptom of wealth, a disease that the affluent West is deeply infected with. What begins as good — pleasure in the extravagance of God's blessings in creation — becomes an orgy of power and control. Peterson describes greed as "using what we have to get more instead of giving away more" (p. 63). The only true wealth we can have is a wealth of grace that we have received and of love that we give. We can never truly be wealthy with power, money, or influence. Just as the parable of the barn builder exposes our greed-wealth, it calls us to a new kind of generosity.

Only the needy are prayerful, which is why the wealthy are so often godless. Therefore, we need a sense of our poverty so that in prayerful humility before God we can discover true wealth.

Quotes for Consideration

"A lot of our talk about 'the things of God' is a way of avoiding the personal presence of God in the hurt and hungry people we meet." (p. 56)

"Nearly all the sins that we get drawn into are packaged as virtues." (p. 58)

"The devil doesn't waste his time tempting us to do something that we know is evil. He hides the evil in something good and then tempts us with the good." (p. 58)

"God does not barely save us, doling out just enough grace to get us across the threshold of heaven. He is lavish." (p. 61)

"Greed is a nearly invisible sin, a tiny parasite that makes its home in the intestines of wealth." (p. 62)

"We quit thinking of wealth as love to be shared and begin calculating it as power to be used." (p. 62)

"Building barns, which is so obviously a good thing, doesn't leave much energy left over for the time-consuming work of loving our neighbors, let alone God." (p. 62)

"Just as idolatry results in a pollution of our love for God, so covetousness results in a pollution of our love for one another. If we keep the first commandment well and the last commandment well, all the commandments between are protected: love God, love your neighbor." (p. 63)

"All our wealth is grace-wealth. We are never power-wealthy, money-wealthy, influence-wealthy. We are love-wealthy." (p. 63)

Questions for Interaction

In what ways does our God-talk inoculate us from dealing with real people with real needs?

What good thing have you done recently that was a disguise for selfishness and sin?

How much of your praying comes out of white-washed selfishness?

How much of your praying is revealing and how much is concealing by what you leave out or emphasize? How does such creative communicating affect our praying and God's responding?

In our affluent, consumer culture, how do we avoid greed? If we can't control it, how do we limit its control of us?

Why is bigger usually not better? Why does more usually leave us with less?

How is greed a form of idolatry, coveting a form of having other gods?

Where in your life are you most poor? Where in your life are you most rich?

How can the affluent foster a sense of neediness before God?

Praying along the Road to Samaria

God of grace, all things are yours and you have no need of anything. Out of your great wealth, you pour out grace upon grace. But in my poverty, I play at wealth, pretending that I am and have all that I need. And yet, in that false wealth, my coveting heart is always wanting more. Show me my real neediness that I may open myself up once again to the abundance of your grace. Through Christ our Lord. Amen.

Manure: Luke 13:6-9

(pp. 65-74)

Theme

Patience, waiting, and quiet in the face of violent haste.

Summary

The threatened violence in the parable of the fruitless fig tree points to the rough conditions of following Jesus. Rejection, opposition, hostility, accusation, violence, and eventually death met Jesus on his path — and that's the same path that we, his followers, tread.

Jesus is a real person, not just some concept behind Christianity. The only way to follow him is by dealing with other real people in real circumstances. Unique relationships. No generalized spirituality. Parables keep us personally engaged with Jesus and others.

Often, personal engagement requires action. But there are many times where it requires restraint. Jesus commands us to go *and* he commands us to stop; knowing when to go and when to stop is essential. But as often as Jesus' commands are disobeyed, his prohibitions are constantly ignored. Doing is easier than not-doing; complacency is overshadowed by impetuosity.

It is more expedient to bulldoze and rebuild than it is to renovate, but Jesus came to save, not bulldoze. And in this parable the saving comes in the form of the earthy, unglamorous spreading of manure. He uses the filth of cows and goats to bring life. Though we are constantly tempted to take shortcuts, to take things into our own hands, God is determined to do things in his way — which just happens to take a lot longer than we'd like it to.

If God isn't in a hurry with people, we shouldn't be either. The way we go about our lives of following Jesus should be congruent with the way God works in the world and in us. Impatience is our greatest temptation. The lesson of the manure points not just to patience but to silence, a waiting that is quiet and watchful. The God who acts is also the God who waits. The God who speaks is also the God who is quiet. And his people are to be like him.

In a messy, violent world that knocks us down and seems to bear little fruit, God's grace and forgiveness are preemptive. And we, who received grace before we knew we needed it, get to get in on extending it to others.

Quotes for Consideration

"Life in the company of Jesus is not a discussion group but an act of becoming." (p. 65)

"If we talk in the company of our friends differently than we talk in the company of Jesus, we desecrate language." (p. 65)

"Following Jesus doesn't make for smooth sailing." (p. 66)

"Religious wars are common and uncommonly bloody. The potential for violence provoked around Jesus is evident from the very beginning." (p. 67)

"There are times when not-doing is commanded, and more often than not it has to do with our intuitively violent response to hostility." (p. 68)

"It is as important not to do what Jesus forbids as it is to obey what he tells us to do." (p. 68)

"Internationally and historically, killing is the predominant method of choice to make the world a better place." (p. 69)

"Manure is a slow solution. Still, when it comes to doing something about what is wrong in the world, Jesus is best known for his fondness for the minute, the invisible, the quiet, the slow — yeast, salt, seeds, light. And manure." (p. 70)

"There are many things that we must not do, *cannot* do, if we are to be faithful to Jesus. Violence is high on the list." (p. 70)

"Silence is the manure of resurrection." (p. 73)

"The farmer's order, 'Chop it down!' is echoed in the Holy Week 'Crucify him!' Jesus' prayer to his Father, 'Forgive them,' is a verbatim repetition of the gardener's intervention, 'Let it alone.'" (p. 74)

Questions for Interaction

Following Jesus may make our lives better, but not easier. In what ways has Jesus made your life better? More difficult or painful?

Do you find it easier to obey Jesus when he *commands* us to do something or when he *forbids* us from doing something? Why?

What are some of Jesus' commands? His prohibitions? Which do you find yourself more willing to obey?

When you find yourself facing significant obstacles in your life — job, marriage, church, friendships, vocation, etc. — do you tend to give them more time, putting in the effort to cultivate them? Or do you chop them down and start over? How will you know if you've worked long enough and cultivated enough before it's time to chop down and start over?

How has your witness to God's grace been undercut by your impetuous actions?

What are you waiting for right now?

When have you received grace before you knew you needed it? In what relationship does someone need to be forgiven by you even though they haven't asked for it?

Praying along the Road to Samaria

How can you be so patient, God? There's so much wrong in the world, so much wrong in my own life. It seems like you could be doing a lot more and doing it a lot faster. But slow me down. Give me patience. Fill me with love and give me the strength to put in the extra work of tending your garden. And thank you for being so patient with me. I wouldn't have survived my own impatience. In the name of the Father and of the Son and of the Holy Spirit. Amen.

SESSION 6

Table Talk: Luke 14:1-14

(pp. 75-84)

Theme

True hospitality is grace in action.

Summary

Hospitality and table talk are central activities in almost every culture. The wideness of Jesus' hospitality to "sinners" made him notorious. While his hospitality drew frowns from others, the lack of hospitality of others drew this chapter's parable.

We all start out life as recipients. Everything is given to us. But as we grow up, we start to take it for granted. God's people become insiders to grace, taking it for granted and not extending it to others.

It is so easy to leave worship in the sanctuary and return to cramped living. Instead of carrying into the rest of life the spaciousness of grace proclaimed and experienced in worship, we become like the small-souled Pharisees that Jesus tangled with.

Hospitality requires humble guests and generous hosts. In the story, the guests are not humble, wrangling for position, and the host is not generous, seeking less to give than to generate obligations. Sabbath is where we learn hospitality, the receiving and the giving of it. But we often betray and desecrate the Sabbath by trying to protect it.

Humble receiving and generous giving are the marks of those who know grace.

Quotes for Consideration

"Eating with 'sinners' became one of the most characteristic and attention-getting facets of Jesus' regular activity." (p. 78)

"Jesus probably has no idea of how to keep Sabbath properly." (p. 80)

"Hospitality is an exercise in humility: when we are guests we are in a position to receive. Hospitality is an exercise in generosity: when we are hosts we are in a position to give." (p. 82)

"Sabbath is the time set aside to do nothing so that we can receive everything." (p. 82)

"Sabbath is the time to receive silence and let it deepen into gratitude, to receive quiet into which forgotten faces and voices unobtrusively make themselves present, to receive the days of the just completed week and absorb the wonder and miracle still reverberating from each one, to receive our Lord's amazing grace." (p. 82)

"Worship is never just worship; meals are never just meals. Holiness permeates hospitality." (p. 83)

Questions for Interaction

With all the grace we receive, how do we maintain a hunger and thirst for righteousness?

Are you a better guest or a better host? Why?

When was the last time you hosted a dinner with guests? How would you describe your hospitality? What is required to be a hospitable host?

When was the last time you were a guest at a meal? How would you describe your host's hospitality? How well did you receive hospitality? What is required to be a hospitable guest?

In what ways is Sabbath a gift of hospitality by God to us? How does it move us from host/doer to guest/receiver?

How hospitable are our congregations to guests? To one another? To God?

The Pharisees in the story betrayed the Sabbath by the way they tried to

protect it. How do we betray Jesus, Scripture, church, worship by the ways we try to protect them?

How would your hospitality change if you were to receive every guest as you would receive Christ?

Jesus was inhospitably treated in this Scripture passage. If he were treated like your average guest, how would you treat him in your home? In your church?

Praying along the Road to Samaria

Holy Trinity, you have invited us into relationship with you — Father, Son, and Holy Spirit — preparing a feast and a home for us with you. In the ultimate act of hospitality, you have adopted us as your own children. Keep us grateful toward you and invitational toward others, passing on the same sort of hospitality that you have extended to us in Jesus. Amen.

The Lost Brothers: Luke 15

(pp. 85-98)

Theme

Regaining a sense of lostness to cure the "cure" of self-righteousness.

Summary

There are times when the cure is more deadly than the malady.

Though we're the community of the saved, the church is filled with spiritually sick people. Righteousness, the sign of health, is conspicuously absent. But the most common cure — self-righteousness — is far more dangerous than the sickness itself. And here's the frustrating thing: if we didn't value righteousness so much, we would never fall into self-righteousness. Our desire to do something good creates a new evil.

The best defense against self-righteousness is a deep awareness of our lost condition. The problem is that we keep getting pats on the back for our self-righteousness, making it that much more difficult to leave aside. The "prodigal son" story is both a cure and a preventative measure against self-righteousness.

Jesus was always on good terms with people on the edge of moral and religious respectability. Whenever we complain of God or anyone else being too gracious, we've stumbled into self-righteousness. It's not the "bad" people who grumble; it's the "good" people.

We murmur when we have a sense of lostness, when the fixed stars we've guided our lives by have shifted. And just as the Hebrews muttered against Moses in the wilderness, it's easy to find ourselves muttering against Jesus because of the road he's taken us on. Instead of all these disreputable people around us, we prefer the security and safety of moralism. If we're lumped in with all these others, there goes our righteousness (our self-righteousness, actually).

In order to unmask our self-righteousness, Jesus tells four (not three) stories of lostness to comprise a single parable.

The first thing we see in the story is the father's passive search for his younger son. Always watching, he waits for the son to take the first step before running to him. This is in contrast with the older son, where the father takes the first step and goes out to find the older son. Discernment is required when deciding whether to wait or act.

The first three stories are built on the same structure: lost, search, found, celebration. The fourth story, the older brother, is incomplete. The self-righteous listeners (which include not just the Pharisees, but us) have been sucked in and are now hit with the bait-and-switch. The parable isn't about all those lost losers; it's about us. The self-righteous are the most lost ones of the bunch. Having lost our sense of lostness, we may never be found. Yes, we are to look for the lost, but we must retain a sense of our own lostness.

Quotes for Consideration

"Not a few of us keep trying to find a way to deal with God without having to pay attention to our neighbors." (p. 87)

"Every sin that originates outside the congregation, sooner or later, shows up within it." (p. 88)

"Self-righteousness is almost never recognized in the mirror. Occasionally in someone else, never in me." (p. 88)

"Only men and women who become Christians are capable of and have the opportunity for some sins, with self-righteousness at the top of the list." (pp. 88-89)

"The people of Israel murmured not because they were bad and evil but because they were good and scared." (p. 93)

"There are situations in which our passivities take precedence over our activities. Waiting provides the time and space for others to get in on salvation." (p. 94)

"The restraint of passivity allows for the quiet, mostly invisible complexities and intricacies that are characteristic of the Holy Spirit as he does his work in us, in the church, in this world for whom Christ died." (p. 95)

"Pharisees are people who have it all together. And what they have together primarily is their religion." (p. 96)

"Self-righteousness in large part consists in a denial of our lostness." (p. 97)

"For as long as we hold on to any pretence of having it all together we are prevented from deepening and maturing in the Christian faith." (p. 98)

"Eusebeigenic sin can be prevented. It is as simple as it is difficult: lay our competencies and skills daily on the altar." (p. 98)

Questions for Interaction

How aware are you of self-righteousness in others? How aware are you of self-righteousness in yourself?

We value righteousness and end up self-righteous instead. How can we help our church be a people who are righteous and not self-righteous?

How does regular confession and a sense of real personal lostness help reduce self-righteousness?

Why do church people tend to focus on the lostness of the "prodigal" son instead of on the lostness of the "good" son? How is the "good" son's lostness more insidious and difficult to deal with than the "prodigal" son's lostness?

The sin of church people is murmuring — grumbling about how God does things, where leadership is taking them, how other people look or act. What are you tempted to grumble about these days?

What hard road is Jesus leading you on right now? What does your grumbling on that road sound like? Who or what are you complaining about?

Have you retained a sense of your own lostness? How has creeping self-righteousness depleted your sense of lostness?

How can we use our skills without letting them dull our sense of lostness?

Praying along the Road to Samaria

Righteous One, we want to be holy like you. But you know what a mess we are and how we trade your grace for a form of self-righteousness, fooling others and ourselves by a polished outward life and religion that is at odds with what we are really like inside. Restore a healthy sense of lostness that we might humbly receive your grace and extend it to all our lost fellows. In Christ our righteousness. Amen.

SESSION 8

The Rascal: Luke 16:1-9

(pp. 99-108)

Theme

The wisdom of throwing ourselves at the Master's mercy and discovering the full extent of his generous grace.

Summary

The parable of the shrewd or crooked manager is one of the most ignored because it seems to encourage bad behavior. But as Peterson writes, "Whatever draws us into these stories it is not moral achievement. These are not stories that goad us to good works" (p. 101). Instead, they are grace stories, stories that get us into who God is and what he is inviting us into. "The stories leave us not with an agenda to do something to make up for whatever we have done wrong, but with an invitation to receive everything from One who wills our wholeness, our well-being" (p. 101).

The rascal in the story is guilty and unexcused. He's fired, but not punished. In fact, other than losing his job, he gets off scot-free through the mercy of the master. The whole story is built on the rock-solid foundation of the master's mercy. Without real mercy from the master and without an *expectation* of that mercy, the rest of the story is impossible, both beginning and end.

The mercy of the master is matched by the prudence or wisdom of the manager. Biblical wisdom and prudence are far from the stodgy, boring, restrained life that comes to our modern minds. Wisdom is a "lifetime of attentiveness to the ways of God" (p. 106) that enlarges our lives, rather than squandering or stifling them. In the parable, after years of watching the mercy of the master, the manager finally discovers the full extent of the master's generosity by throwing himself fully into it.

As he tells the story, Jesus revives our vocabulary. Grace-words often become dull and dead over time as they get squeezed and choked into smaller and smaller definitions. It is through stories like this that they spring to new life again.

Quotes for Consideration

"The story about the rascal describes the behavior of a man who narrowly escapes a lifetime of self-serving calculation and discovers himself reveling in a huge world of generosity — of God." (p. 106)

"Novelists always have a much more difficult time making a good person attractive and interesting than they do a scoundrel or a rogue." (p. 106)

"The generous action of God defines his life, not his obsessive scheming, embezzling, and cooking the books." (p. 107)

"Words wear out. They lose texture, and colors fade. They need refurbishing, rehabilitating, renovating." (p. 107)

"Jesus manages to get these words [like "prudent"] alive and kicking again, not by sending us a dictionary and tracing their origins, but by putting them in a story where we can't miss the robust nature that bursts out in surprised response to Jesus." (p. 108)

Questions for Interaction

What do you think of when you hear the word "prudence"? How about "wisdom"? Are these words you would use to characterize your own life? Why or why not?

"Jesus came to save our souls. He also came to save our words" (p. 107). What Christian words (like "wisdom" and "prudence") have lost their flavor and sound dull or irrelevant? Make a list — "repentance," "obedience," "reconciliation," etc. Give each of them a dull definition and then see if you can come up with stories like this parable to make each of them come alive and sing again.

How does this parable rehabilitate the words "wisdom" and "prudence"?

Have you ever thrown yourself fully on the mercy and generosity of God like the rascal in the parable? If not, why not? If so, what did you expect and what did you in fact experience?

Praying along the Road to Samaria

Merciful Master, you have always stood ready to give grace generously. But even though I've needed it, I've rarely asked for it. Grow in me the wisdom of a lifelong attentiveness to you and your ways that I might know and trust you enough to throw myself into the kindness of your mercy. In Jesus, who makes your mercy shine. Amen.

The Invisible Man: Luke 16:19-31

(pp. 109-21)

Theme

Repentance orients us to the kingdom of God, opening our eyes to the invisibles.

Summary

The phrase "a certain man" links this parable to the two preceding it. In each, the story was heading south, but then a "visitation of grace reverses the plotline" (p. 110). The Lazarus story is not a fable about the afterlife — that's merely the setting. It is a repentance story in line with the two stories before.

Lazarus is an invisible man to everyone except Jesus, who names him. But the wealthy man around whom everyone crowded remains unnamed. In his naming and not-naming, Jesus paints a whole new order of things. God sees those we don't see and overlooks those we focus on. This is part of the "great reversal" of the kingdom of God.

All stories are part of a larger meta-story. Some stories are trivial, but real stories point to something bigger, a larger reality.

After making invisible Lazarus visible, Jesus turns his attention to the rich man's brothers, the real focus of the story. Resurrection is taking place all around Jesus, people are coming to life, but it requires repentance to get in on it. An easy word to understand but a difficult word to hear, repentance is less an individualistic self-improvement life change than turning to join the people of God in following his ways. Although personal change takes place, repentance is not about private salvation, but about orienting to God's kingdom.

Imperatives get us moving. Stories pull us into life. There is a place for imperatives: we need to get moving. But stories provide the shape and substance for a life. Imperatives work well only in the context of stories.

Quotes for Consideration

"We put our sick in hospitals, our elderly in nursing homes, our poor in slums, and our garbage in landfills." (p. 113)

"By and large, by averting our gaze, tuning out the sounds, and sanitizing the environment, we manage pretty well not to see or hear or smell or touch Lazarus." (p. 113)

"[This is] not a story about what happens after we die, but a story that is repeated with variations all around us every day." (p. 114)

"Jesus lays the groundwork for inclusiveness among the 'whosoever' by naming the unnamed, making visible those whom no one sees, giving voice to the ones who are never listened to." (p. 115)

"Jesus is on the hunt for followers who will participate with him in establishing his kingdom rule. His first recruits take most bystanders by surprise." (p. 115)

"Story is a verbal witness to the coherence of life, the interconnectedness of beginning, middle, and end." (p. 115)

"Story enlists our imagination to grasp more than our immediate feelings and surroundings — other lives, other circumstances, other possibilities." (p. 116)

"In the biblical story repentance cannot be narrowed down to something private, such as being sorry for your sins and ready to make amends. The call is to return to God and the ways of God with his people." (pp. 118-19)

"What I am trying to get a feel for is that while imperatives are absolutely essential for getting our attention and getting us doing or not doing something, they don't function as intended until they get us into the story." (p. 120)

Questions for Interaction

Why is Lazarus named and not the rich man, when it's the rich man, not Lazarus, who does the speaking and acting?

Although named by Jesus, Lazarus is an invisible man to everyone else. Who are the invisible people in our culture? In your church? In your family? What can help open our eyes to those we've been trained to ignore?

What do you find more effective in the short term: an imperative that gets you going or a story that captures your imagination? What is more effective in the long term? How do the two work together?

Peterson shifts the emphasis of repentance away from the merely personal toward a communal participation in the kingdom of God. How does an individual focus keep us from true repentance? How does a kingdom perspective differ from a personal righteousness perspective?

How is the Lazarus story really about the rich man's brothers?

Praying along the Road to Samaria

Lord, nothing and no one escapes your gaze. But my eyes get so filled with all the bluff and bluster of this world that I miss out on so much and so many. I turn my eyes to you. Open them to you and your kingdom and all those who have been invisible to me to this point. In Jesus. Amen.

The Widow: Luke 18:1-8

(pp. 122-32)

Theme

Sometimes our imaginations need to be shocked back into thinking rightly about God so that we don't give up on praying to him.

Summary

"Pray" makes a great verb, but "prayer" makes a lousy noun. Praying is something to do, not something to talk or read about. Since prayer is a verbal noun — a noun that has no meaning apart from action — it is no wonder that there is a lot of praying (action) within the pages of Scripture but hardly anything said about prayer (praying that has been stopped, dissected, and abstracted).

Jesus tells a prayer story, teaching on prayer without ever becoming abstract. In it, a widow is defrauded and has no one to stand for her. In fact, the judge ignores her, just as he has ignored God and everyone else. But she doesn't quit. She beats him up with badgering. And so he relents, giving her what she wants.

Everyone prays. Many give up. God doesn't seem to care or listen, like a bad judge.

God's silence is the common experience of God's people. It is not a matter of our personal inadequacy or bad technique. Our consistent witness to this are the prayers collected in the Psalms. This witness points not only to God's silence but also to the perseverance of his people in their praying.

The biblical revelation of God is what keeps us praying. We've come to know his character through the vast story of God in Scripture. But sometimes we get sucked into thinking badly about him. Maybe he's like a bad judge, unscrupulous and uninterested in justice. But then Jesus tells this parable and we're shocked, scandalized almost. This judge is nothing like the God we've come to know. In fact, the contrast helps reboot our imaginations.

And our imaginations need rebooting in order to see and get in on the kingdom of God that Jesus is proclaiming and enacting. So Jesus uses shocking, apocalyptic language to jump-start our flat imaginations so that we can understand the urgency of the kingdom of God. The way he uses apocalyptic language has little to do with the future and everything to do with waking up to the kingdom coming right here and now.

In a haywire world, an apocalyptic imagination keeps us praying, keeps us participating in the kingdom of God, keeps us from giving up when we don't see things going our way in the world, keeps us persistent like the widow.

Quotes for Consideration

"In the biblical story there is very little, if any, interest in prayer as a thing in itself." (p. 122)

"They don't take time out to pray. Praying is what they are doing as they are preparing, as they are following." (p. 122)

"All prayer is embedded in person and place and time. It is not the kind of thing that can be approached as an abstraction." (p. 122)

"Prayer is not an option; it is fundamentally necessary. Prayer is not a pious interlude; it necessarily permeates life at all times and places." (p. 123)

"Most people, maybe all, at one time or another, pray. And many — who knows how many? — quit. . . . The remarkable thing about prayer is not that so many people pray, but that some of us keep at it. Why do we keep at it? Why do we keep praying when we have so little to show for it?" (p. 125)

"God's silence in the face of our prayers is not due to some inadequacy on our part. . . . God's silence is a common and repeated experience among all who pray." (p. 125)

"People who pray ask 'How long?' and 'Why?' a lot." (p. 127)

"The sketch of the evil judge in Jesus' story is everything that we know God is *not*. . . . [T]his judge is an evil and grotesque parody of the God who is revealed to us." (p. 128)

"Kingdom is what is going on all the time, whether we are aware of it or not." (p. 129)

"Kingdom requires a total renovation of our imagination so that we are able to see what our eyes do not see, so that we are capable of participating in what will not be reported in tomorrow morning's newspaper." (p. 129)

"Apocalyptic is a language for breaking open awareness of the tremendous energies of good and evil contending with one another beneath the apparently benign skin of the ordinary. The language of apocalyptic vision calls the praying imagination into vigorous participation in what God is doing right now." (p. 131)

Questions for Interaction

Have you read any books on prayer? Have they been helpful or have they actually made praying more abstract and difficult? How so?

How do you feel about your praying?

When have you grown discouraged in praying because of the lack of an answer?

Have you ever felt or been told that God didn't answer your prayer because of some inadequacy in you? How does this stand against the biblical witness?

What is the kingdom of God that Jesus proclaimed — not just as a future reality but as already in our midst?

When you look around you, do you see the kingdom of God or do you see your life and the rest of the world just slowly passing by?

Have you ever persisted in disobedient prayer? How is that different from obedient persistence in prayer? What signs signify the difference between the two?

Praying along the Road to Samaria

God of revelation, you have revealed yourself in Scripture and most fully in Jesus, the Word. And yet you are so quiet I sometimes wonder if you are listening, and I begin to question your goodness. Shock my imagination with apocalyptic that I might see your kingdom and hear your voice and never give up praying to you. In the name of the Lamb who was slain. Amen.

The Sinners: Luke 18:9-14

(pp. 133-44)

Theme

Hypocrisy kills our faith and prayers. We need the company of honest sinners.

Summary

Just as most of an iceberg is below the waterline, most of what is going on in people and in the world around us is invisible. Storytellers open our eyes to what is really going on.

When Jesus tells stories, he does so to open our eyes. But he's not content with just that. He wants to get us in on what he's opening our eyes to. Abstract truth is nothing. He's after participation.

Jesus tells a story of two men at prayer. Both in worship, both sinners. One, a Pharisee, has a good opinion of himself; the other, a tax collector, has a bad opinion of himself. Just like the people in our pews each Sunday, we have our people who take God and his laws seriously and we have our unscrupulous characters. But the obviously godly man isn't what he seems. He's a fake, a hypocrite.

Prayer and the place of prayer are magnets for hypocrisy. Not only are there plenty of benefits from seeming close to God, but it's easy to fake. The problem is that hypocrisy paralyzes the life of faith and prayer. Too much church, therefore, can be deadly to our souls.

Hypocrisy is a slow-growing cancer. It's a lazy replacement of an interior that chases after God with an exterior that only seems to. No one ever sets out to be a hypocrite, but many end up there.

Both men in Jesus' story are sinners. One knows it and one doesn't. One sins outwardly and gets glared at for it — inside and outside match. One sins inwardly and gets pats on the back for it — inside and outside don't match.

Pharisees (that is, church people) are good people. Pharisee ≠ hypocrite. They have an appetite for righteousness, but their religious environment is a greenhouse for hypocrisy. They need vigilance to keep from falling into it. But often it's the prayers and faith of the rough-cut new Christians who show up every now and then that keep them from hypocrisy. The simplicity of their prayers and their fresh experiences of grace return us to renewed simplicity.

Quotes for Consideration

"Jesus does not tell stories in order to illustrate large 'truths' about God and salvation, the devil and damnation." (p. 134)

"Nothing is more rudely dismissive of Jesus than to treat him as a Sunday school teacher who shows up on Sundays to teach us about God and how to stay out of trouble." (p. 135)

"People go to church for many of the wrong reasons. The right reason for going to church is to pray . . . cultivating an attentive listening and speaking relation to the God who listens and speaks." (p. 138)

"While there are visible and audible words involved in prayer, prayer is mostly an interior act, the most interior act, in fact, that humans can engage in." (p. 138)

"No one can tell just by observing whether a person using the forms and words of prayer is actually praying." (p. 138)

"How easy it is to acquire a reputation as a man or a woman who is on good terms with God without bothering to pay attention to God, how easy it is to use the setting of church and the forms and words of prayer to avoid the demanding work of dealing with God." (p. 139)

"Hypocrisy is a unique sin in that it does not begin in a temptation to do wrong. . . . Hypocrisy originates in a place of prayer and with people who pray." (p. 139).

"[Hypocrisy] is the lazy replacement of a strenuous interior life with God with religious makeup and gossipy god-chatter." (p. 140)

"Prayer is not a mystical or esoteric piece of spirituality. It is ordinary. Prayer is not a technique you can learn. . . . It is as simple as an act of friendship." (p. 143)

"In prayer we persistently, faithfully, trustingly come before God, submitting ourselves to his sovereignty, confident that he is acting, right now, on our behalf." (p. 144)

Questions for Interaction

"The right reason to go to church is to pray" (p. 138). What are some other reasons we go to church? How do those pull us away from the "right reason" to go to church? How much of what goes on at church is prayer?

It is easy to "pray" without actually praying, without listening and speaking to the God who listens and speaks to us. How much of your praying is actual praying? How much has the form of praying but never engages with God?

Does your public praying match your alone praying?

Spiritual hypocrisy is easy to hide. In what ways have you slipped into it?

Hypocrisy is difficult to self-diagnose. Do you have someone or a group of someones whose job it is to be honest with you, helping you to unmask your creeping hypocrisies? If not, who might you go to? If so, what was the last thing they unmasked?

Familiarity breeds contempt. How might too much church activity actually be deadening to faith and prayer?

Who do you know well whose hypocrisy is vividly evident? How can you kindly and appropriately show true friendship by steering them back to genuine God-pursuit?

In what ways do our Pharisee church cultures keep tax collectors from becoming a part of our congregations?

How have the fresh and gritty prayers of young or unschooled Christians pulled you back from hypocrisy, refreshing your determination to follow Jesus?

Praying along the Road to Samaria

So, God, here we go again, confessing our sins once again, wishing that we didn't need too, often pretending that we didn't need to. But Lord, you know how many times I've prayed without even praying but simply going through the motions. Is it because I'm hiding from you — or hiding from myself? Unmask my hypocrisies and surround me with honest sinners that I might rediscover honest grace. Amen.

The Minimalist: Luke 19:11-27

(pp. 145-55)

Theme

Investing in the kingdom is required, and it's done through the storied words we speak.

Summary

We are strangers in a strange land. We live in a world, in a culture that may speak of "God" but know nothing of the way of Jesus and the kingdom of God he proclaimed. We walk a Samaritan road. The problem is that we can seem pretty Samaritan ourselves. So Jesus slips stories in past our defenses, telling it slant, conditioning us to the kingdom without our even being aware of it.

The central theme of the biblical story is this: "God wants us; we don't want God" (p. 149). He pursues us like a lover in order to conceive a new life in us, his own life. All the initiative in our relationship with him comes from his side. But we're not all that interested. We'd prefer to be our own gods, although on occasion we'll invent other gods when we need them. Gods on our own terms. Gods our size. But we always become like the gods we make and serve: lifeless. (Given our predisposition for god-making, it's no wonder people don't gravitate to the kingdom of God.)

When the king in the parable entrusts his servants with money to invest, he expects them to do it in the way he would and on his behalf. Some do, but a play-it-safe minimalist doesn't. And the king is angry.

Jesus is serious about investing in, building his kingdom. But he wants it done in his way. And that's the way of stories, not swords. All of the stories that have been told up to this point are the coins to be invested, the ways Jesus is bringing about the kingdom. They aren't to be buried; they're to be told, spread out, put to good use. Non-participation is disobedience. There is too much at stake.

Quotes for Consideration

"We don't come to God; God comes to us. We don't start the conversation; God starts it." (p. 150)

"God is a rival, not an ally, in the god-business. We want to be our own gods. . . . As it turns out, we are very good at it." (p. 150)

"The naiveté that assumes that if we just make Jesus more attractive men and women will flock in great numbers and follow him is astonishing. The widespread American assumption that if we can just get the gospel message out loud and clear men and women will sign up on the spot is an illusion of the Snake." (p. 151)

"From now on it was stories, not swords, that would form the identity of the followers of Jesus and provide the content and shape of the kingdom in which they were citizens." (p. 153)

"The story is unrelenting: self-serving minimalism is not an option. There are no non-participants in Jesus' kingdom." (p. 155)

"More space is given to the judgment delivered on the play-it-safe, cautious, non-participating, non-servant than the other nine servants." (p. 155)

Questions for Interaction

How do we talk about the kingdom of God in an American culture that is all about the kingdom of self?

Peterson writes: "America leads the world at present in golden-calf production" (p. 151). Is this true? If so, how is it true? What kinds of gods do we make?

What kinds of not-gods are you most tempted to serve?
How is Jesus' kingdom different from other kingdoms?
Do you play it safe with what God has entrusted you?
Jesus builds his kingdom with stories. How have they built his kingdom
    in you? How have you used them to build his kingdom in others?

Praying along the Road to Samaria

God of history, your saving love is the plot of humanity's story.
Keep me in the middle of your story and boldly sharing your
story with others. In Jesus. Amen.

PART II

Jesus in His Prayers

Keeping Company with Jesus as He Prays: Six Prayers

(pp. 159-66)

Summary

While stories keep us concretely connected to people and the details of our lives, prayers keep us "answeringly attentive" to the God who speaks to us. Down-to-earth stories lead to down-to-earth praying. Nothing abstract. Nothing impersonal. And in an era of abstract, impersonal spiritualities, we need the protection of Jesus' stories and prayers. That is why the vast majority of our Scriptures are story and prayer.

Silence is just as important to our praying as is our speaking, keeping us listening and keeping us from babbling.

Prayer is not only the easiest thing to do — we all pray — but it is also the easiest thing to fake. So, when we get stuck, we resort to set prayers, to the Psalms and to Jesus' prayers. The prayers of Jesus keep us honest, attentive, responsive, and participating in what God is doing. Without his help, we would end up with scraps of prayers and nothing of much consequence.

But Jesus does more than just teach us how to pray. He prays. The Jesus who prayed in the Gospels is the one who is praying for us right now. When we don't know what to pray, he's praying for us. When we don't know how to pray, he's praying for us.

The prayers Jesus prayed give a shape to our praying. The prayers Jesus prays right now give substance to our praying.

Quotes for Consideration

"Prayer is anemic if the language dissipates into mist, into a pious fog of sentimentalities, thinned out to pious clichés." (p. 160)

"Story and prayer are the core language of our humanity. We say most truly who we are when we tell stories to one another and pray to our Lord." (p. 160)

"Silence, which in prayer consists mostly in attentive listening, is non-negotiable. Listening, which necessarily requires silence on our part, is as much a part of language as words." (p. 160)

"More often than not, silence gets short shrift in our prayers. Yet if there is no silence, our speech degenerates into babble." (p. 160)

"Prayer is our first language. Anybody can pray. And everybody does. We pray even when we don't know we are praying." (p. 161)

"Jesus is our master in prayer; he is also our companion in prayer." (p. 163)

"Jesus prays. He is praying for us right now. He was praying for us yesterday. He will be praying for us tonight as we sleep and tomorrow morning as we wake up. Jesus praying for us is a current event." (p. 164)

"Prayer is the language of the Trinity, intimately personal." (p. 165)

Questions for Interaction

What is appealing about techniques or formulas for praying? How can they be helpful? How can they be harmful?

Is your praying more like a gathering of scraps or like singing?

We don't just pray to Jesus, he prays for us. How does the fact that Jesus is praying for you *right now* change the way you pray yourself?

Why don't we have more of Jesus' prayers in the Gospels? Why might it be good that we have some, but not too many?

Praying with Jesus

Jesus, thank you for praying for me, and with me, right now. Open up a praying heart in me so that my scraps of prayers become more like singing. Amen.

Jesus Prays with Us: Matthew 6:9-13

(pp. 167-96)

Summary

The Sermon on the Mount is the center of Jesus' teaching. The Lord's Prayer is the center of the sermon. Prayer is the beating heart of the kingdom of God. Without it, rest in peace.

Our Father in heaven. The personal, relational metaphor helps retain the personal, relational nature of prayer and keeps it from devolving into technique. "Father" keeps us from functionalizing God, from reducing him to what we can get from him. Intimacy, not formality.

Hallowed be your name. God has a name: Yahweh. He's not an idea. He is a person to be related to. But not to cozy up to. He is holy, different, other. There is a childlike intimacy that we get in on with God but that also includes deep reverence. Affectionate awe.

Your kingdom come. "Kingdom" defines reality in relationship to God. Prayer, too. It declares by its simple action that all things have to do with God. Our praying draws us into the kingdom work that Jesus was about. God hasn't given up his throne. He intends to be King, but he invites us to help bring about his rule. He (not the newspapers) defines his kingdom and determines how it comes to be. He brings it in his way, which includes crosses and prayers.

Your will be done. The will of God isn't a *thing* out there, as some make it out to be. It has to do with the relationship our personal God has with real persons. It has to do with God's energies bringing his purposes to be.

On earth as it is in heaven. Prayer brings our world together with the world of God, making the two one.

Give us this day our daily bread. We're no angels. Unlike angels, we have bodies. And bodies require food and other mundane physical things. Praying for "bread" is an embrace of our physicality and of our dogged dependence on others, primarily God. We have a basic neediness that doesn't have to do with stuff. But consumerism gives us the idea that we can get everything we need, and money and technology seem to give us the power to do so. The limits that our needs bring protect our creatureliness, our not-Godness.

And forgive us our debts, as we forgive our debtors. There are more than fifty Hebrew words for sin. We're good at taking and breaking, violence and manipulation. Jesus doesn't tell us how to fix ourselves or others. Instead, he teaches us to forgive and pray for forgiveness. When we sin, part of us dies. Forgiveness is a form of resurrection, bringing us back to life again.

And lead us not into temptation, but deliver us from evil. Save us from the unknown — that which lurks within and without. We live in a dangerous world; we need help. The problem is that temptation and evil rarely look like themselves; they dress up like the good, the true, and the beautiful. So we're praying to avoid the seemingly good so that we can do the truly good. We have a bent toward sin that teaching and training in moral behavior can reduce but just can't stop. Our natural goodness is the very area where the most subtle and deceptive temptations arise.

For yours is the kingdom, and the power, and the glory, for ever. Amen. We pray, handing our concerns to God, and we're done. Everything is up to him now. We've relinquished all pretense at control.

The Lord's Prayer provides an embroidery hoop for our souls, giving our limp souls a tautness that allows God to do his fine needlework.

Quotes for Consideration

"A kingdom-of-heaven life consists of things to do and ways to think, but
    if there is no prayer at the center nothing lives." (p. 167)
"'Father' is Jesus' metaphor of choice for God. Get used to this: *Father.* The
    oldest and most implacable enemy in the practice of prayer is de-
    personalization, turning prayer into a technique, using prayer as a
    device." (p. 169)

50

"Prayer is not passive. Prayer is not resignation. God is active. As Jesus prays he enters the action of God. As he prays with us, he implicitly invites us into the action. As we pray with him we volunteer ourselves into the action." (p. 171)

"Holiness is the distinctive quality of otherness that sets God beyond and apart from — *other than* — us. God is not like us. We are not like God. . . . We don't begin by getting cozy with God. We begin with solemn reverence: Holy." (pp. 171-72)

"The kingdom of God that Jesus announces as present here and now is not a religious piece of the world pie that God takes a special interest in. . . . There is no other world. . . . Nothing takes place outside the kingdom of God." (p. 175)

"God is not president or prime minister of a democracy. God is king. . . . It is a sovereignty that invites our participation. We share his rule, but it is *his* rule." (p. 175)

"The kingdom we pray for can never be grasped by what we read in the newspapers or in the history books. . . . But it can be discerned by means of our prayers." (p. 176)

"The phrase 'will of God' may well be one of the murkiest set of words in the Christian vocabulary." (p. 179)

"Heaven and earth are distinct but not separate. Heaven and earth are an organic unity." (p. 181)

"Prayer is not an escape from what is going on around us. It is gutsy participation in every earthly detail." (p. 181)

"Consumerism is a narcotic that dulls the awareness that we are in need. By buying what we need, we assume control of our lives. Technology is a narcotic. It depersonalizes needs to something that can be handled by a machine or a device." (p. 183)

"Needs prepare us for a life of receptivity, a readiness to receive what can only be received as a gift." (p. 184)

"Limits don't limit us from being fully human. They only limit us from being God. . . . Do we want to live without limits? Then we want to live without God." (p. 184)

"God does not deal with sin by ridding our lives of it. . . . God deals with sin by forgiving us, and when he forgives us there is more of us, not less." (p. 186)

"Part of us dies when we sin. . . . The only way to deal with sin is by resurrection. Forgiveness is resurrection, life from the dead." (p. 188)

"Jesus does not teach us about prayer, he prays with us; we do not learn about prayer, we pray with him." (p. 189)

"Temptation and evil almost always appear disguised as good and beautiful. . . . The garden temptation is all about participating in an illusory good." (p. 191)

"Forgiveness is the only known way of restoring the relationship, the personal dimensions of intimacy with God and one another that are at the core of our humanity." (p. 192)

Questions for Interaction

Prayer is never solitary. Even when we're alone, we pray with Jesus and his followers. How does this ever-communal nature change your praying?

What name/term/relationship do you regularly use to address God in prayer (for example, "Gracious God," "Lord," "Creator," "Father God," etc.)? How does this shape your prayers? How might different names shape your view of and relationship with God?

Do you refer to God as "Father" in your praying?

Has the word "Father" retained its relational nature in your praying or has it, too, become an abstract title? How do you safeguard the Father-child nature of your praying from slipping into the address of a titled deity?

"Prayer is not passive" (p. 171). Do you feel like you've actually *done* something when you've prayed? How might our prayers be more important than most of our actions?

Do you have reverence for God's name or do you glibly toss it around? How can you bring intimacy and reverence together in the way you use God's name?

Peterson writes, "Prayer involves us deeply and responsibly in all the operations of God" (p. 182). Is it true that we can be involved in *everything* God does through prayer? How does that shape your approach to praying?

Peterson writes that prayer "involves God deeply and transformatively in all the details of our lives" (p. 182). Does that deep and transformative involvement make you more anxious or more excited? Explain.

Which would you rather be: totally sinless or totally forgiven? Why?

What is the worst part of sin?

Peterson writes, "We don't sin against a commandment; we sin against a person" (p. 187). Is this true? Is this how you live?

When have you found yourself participating in something evil when you thought you were participating in something good?

What good characteristic are you most known for? What subtle temptations arise for you in this area?

Whom do you need to forgive? What is holding you back from forgiving this person? What will remain dead in you until you do forgive?

Have you seen an admirable quality in someone over time slowly become a means for wrongdoing? Have you seen the same in yourself?

Praying with Jesus

Our Father, who art in heaven, hallowed be your Name. Your kingdom come, your will be done on earth as it is in heaven. Give us this day our daily bread. Forgive us our debts as we forgive our debtors. And lead us not into temptation but deliver us from evil. For thine is the kingdom and the power and the glory forever. Amen.

Jesus Prays in Thanksgiving: Matthew 11:25-26

(pp. 197-203)

Summary

Jesus' thanksgiving prayer comes out of being misunderstood and ignored. John the baptizer, his cousin, had helped launch Jesus' ministry, but he misunderstood what Jesus was about. John had launched a big impact ministry and handed it off to Jesus only to see nothing happen. And the people in the villages who knew Jesus best, who saw him doing amazing signs and wonders, ignored him.

These are no conditions to account for Jesus' thankfulness. If anything, they are the conditions of frustration. But Jesus isn't unsettled by the conditions. He takes them seriously, confronting and rebuking, but he never despairs. Instead, we see thanksgiving, a sense of God that spills out on everything else, eyes that see all the hidden actions of the Father.

Quotes for Consideration

"John and Jesus were different in the ways they went about their work. John preached in thunder to popular acclaim; Jesus told stories over meals and with friends on the road. John was a public figure confronting the high-profile sin of Herod Antipas in the public square; Jesus worked for the most part inconspicuously in the small villages in Galilee. . . . It is understandable that John might be offended at Je-

54

sus' ways of going about his messianic work. Where is the 'increase' that John was expecting?" (p. 199)

"All of these villages were within walking distance of each other. They were all small villages, villages in which virtually everyone would be known and recognized. No one in a small town is anonymous. No one would have been ignorant of Jesus. All would know the stories of his healings. Many would have heard him preach and teach. Many — perhaps most — ignored him." (p. 200)

"Willful indifference to God is the worst thing. A steely refusal to repent, to stubbornly persist in a complacent, self-satisfied life, is a doomed life." (p. 200)

"Pollsters, who love to inform the world on the statistical status of God, have no prophetic credibility in kingdom matters." (p. 202)

"Hidden kingdom energies surge just beneath the surface all around us." (p. 202)

Questions for Interaction

Do you, like John the baptizer, sometimes wish Jesus would be a bit more obvious in what he's doing? In what ways would you like to see more obvious action from Jesus? How might that be a misunderstanding of who Jesus is and what he's about?

When have you been disappointed with God? In what ways are you disappointed with the church, God's chosen way of working in the world?

Public opinion polls always show a high level of respect for Jesus, and yet the same people are basically indifferent to him. Why is this? Why is it that many who attend churches are basically indifferent to Jesus, rarely praying?

Do you feel more thankful to God during times of abundance and success or during times of emptiness and need? Why?

Why do we seem to be less grateful with much and more grateful with little?

How can too much good — too much worship, Scripture, churchy stuff — actually anesthetize us to God?

How can familiarity lead to disobedience?

Jesus wasn't discouraged by the indifference of local Jewish villagers. How do you react to the indifference of Christians in church pews?

How much impact does Christian apathy really have on the kingdom of
   God?

Take some time to look for prayer and holiness that are actually taking
   place in the midst of all the misunderstanding and indifference that
   seem so obviously to negate the kingdom of God. How much is
   there? More or less than you expected?

Praying with Jesus

I thank you, Father, Lord of heaven and earth, because you have
hidden these things from the wise and the intelligent and have
revealed them to infants; yes, Father, for such was your gracious
will. Amen.

SESSION 16

Jesus Prays in Anticipation of the End: John 12:27-28

(pp. 204-11)

Summary

"Father, glorify your name" is the simple prayer of Jesus soon before his crucifixion. It's a prayer that conjures up images of magnificence, of God, or something that will transform and enliven us if we encounter it, if we encounter the Glory.

But Jesus redefines glory in terms of his death and burial, being crowned and hailed as king on the way to the cross. The way we get in on the glory is the same — not by grasping, but by letting go, receiving our lives by giving them up. We can get in on the glory by choosing to die now (not that this is easy!). Just as Jesus was tempted to pray to be saved from the painful hour of glory, we naturally turn away from it ourselves. But instead of praying for himself, Jesus prayed that the Father's name would be glorified.

There is nothing "glorious" in this kind of glory — no glamour, no praise, no great show of strength. But it is glorious in showing the great love of God and in its participation in the salvation of the world. That's real glory that we can get in on.

Quotes for Consideration

"All of life, human life, is sacramental, a container for and revelation of the holy: the Word." (p. 204)

"Metaphors are to be taken seriously and not reduced to a 'meaning' or a
 'truth.'" (p. 205)
"Prayer is not a subject of its own." (p. 206)
"Prayer is not something we pull out of the web of revelation and incar-
 nation and then sign on to be 'prayer warriors.'" (p. 207)
"We can't comprehend glory in bits and pieces; we need the Story from
 Beginning to Ending, from Birth to Death and Beyond." (p. 207)
"Glory is not just more of what I already have, or the perfection of what I
 already see." (p. 209)
"We don't have to wait until we die before we die. We don't have to wait
 until after our funerals to get in on the glory." (p. 209)
"It wasn't exactly easy for Jesus to redefine glory so that it included loss,
 rejection, and death." (p. 210)
"We must let Jesus daily redefine the word 'glory' or we will miss it en-
 tirely." (p. 210)
"The glory with which Jesus is glorified is not inspirational." (p. 211)
"Jesus is the dictionary in which we look up the meaning of words."
 (p. 211)

Questions for Interaction

How would you define the word "glory"?
How does the "glory" of Jesus compare and differ from the glory our culture is enamored with?
Peterson asks, "Do I think that prayer is a kind of mechanism, like a car
 jack, that I use to lever myself to a higher plane where I have better
 access to God?" (p. 209). When have you encountered this kind of
 approach to prayer in others? In yourself?
In what relationship is Jesus calling you to take up your cross so that the
 Father's name (not yours) will be glorified in your "dying"?

Praying with Jesus

Father, glorify your Name.

Jesus Prays for Us: John 17

(pp. 212-30)

Summary

The night before his death, Jesus prays for his disciples (John 17). It is an upside-down evening, with Jesus saying and doing (for example, washing feet) things that point to his upside-down way of being king of a kingdom that is very upside-down from the way we think of kings and kingdoms. When we get to John 17, the rush of questions has hushed and prayer has begun. Quiet and holy listening, the prerequisites of prayer, fill the room.

Jesus praying for us — now, not just then — is the main context for our lives, every aspect and moment of our lives. Our prayers are never first but join with Jesus in his praying.

The word "glory," already big in John's Gospel, comes to a crescendo in Jesus' prayer and the events afterward. We are oriented to the upside-down glory of Jesus' death.

If we ever doubted that prayer is personal, relational speech (not abstract or formal), Jesus' prayer is conclusive. The personal dominates. This is completely relational language to the Father Jesus loves and for the disciples he loves. Jesus wants us in on all that God is and says and does. He wants us to be one with the Trinity.

The track record of twenty centuries of Christianity seems to prove Jesus' prayer for unity a failure. Those who try to create unity usually do so either by coercion (institution) or by dividing into groups of personal preference (schism). But unity exists, and it transcends institutional bounds and sectarian divisions. It is slow, but it is having its way with us.

Peterson writes, "The 'one' that Jesus is praying us into is the One who is the Trinity. This 'one' is truly one, but it is a one that gathers all particularities into a relational unity" (p. 226).

Sin isolates; love unites. But love cannot reach its goal of unity through sin's method of coercion. Freedom is required, and that means freedom to reject love. The only way to experience the unity Jesus prayed for is to freely enter into the life and relationship of the Trinity. The unity Jesus prayed for is not a command, because we can't do it. Only he can pull it off.

Quotes for Consideration

"God cannot be rushed into human hearts. A life of love and obedience can't be rushed into human hearts." (p. 213)

"We seldom know enough to ask the right questions. In the company of Jesus we learn not to insist on answers to our questions — we learn to let Jesus carry the conversation where he wills." (p. 216)

"Being prayed for is also an element in the life of prayer — a very large part, but often largely underappreciated. When it is Jesus who is praying for us, being prayed for may well be the largest part of prayer." (p. 217)

"Glory is not only what dazzles the eye but what illuminates the believing heart. Glory expands inward. It comprehends a revealed reality that works invisibly from beneath, infusing life from below." (p. 219)

"There is nothing quite as destructive to the gospel of Jesus Christ as the use of language that dismisses the way Jesus talks and prays and takes up instead the rhetoric of smiling salesmanship or vicious invective." (p. 220)

"Prayer is not a distancing operation. Prayer is not a religious exercise that 'puts things in perspective' or 'puts people in their place.' It is involving." (p. 221)

"Jesus' prayer is not about ideas or projects; it is personal involvement in all the operations of the Trinity." (p. 221)

"Don't miss this: Father, Son, and every last one of us by the prayer and the cross of Jesus and the work of the Holy Spirit are made one." (p. 223)

"The Christian church is famous worldwide for being contentious and mean-spirited, for using the words of Moses and Jesus as weapons to exclude and condemn." (p. 223)

"It may be slow in coming, but Jesus' prayer will have its way with us." (p. 225)

"The longer we stay in Jesus' praying presence the more we will understand that our impulses toward schism and sectarianism, our rivalries and denunciations, have no place in the room while Jesus is praying for us 'to be one.'" (p. 225)

"We cannot become one with one another or with God apart from freedom." (p. 227)

"The church is the large, healthy, Trinitarian gathering ground where we let God be God." (p. 228)

"The church is the primary arena in which we learn that glory does not consist in what we do for God but in what God does for us." (p. 228)

Questions for Interaction

Why is it an important part of our praying to have others pray for us? What are the most difficult parts of being prayed for by others?

Jesus prays for us. What does it mean to be "prayerfully present to the praying Presence" (p. 217)? How can Jesus praying for us be the largest part of our praying?

How does knowing that Jesus prays for us (prays, not just prayed) make you feel? How does/might it shape your own praying, knowing that he is right now praying for us?

Jesus talks the same way with his Father as with his friends. In what ways does your prayer language differ from your everyday language? What would need to change to make them the same?

Jesus prays that we will participate in the very life of the Trinity. Do you know yourself as one with the Trinity? Do you know yourself as one with other Christians (who are themselves one with the Trinity)? How would the way you live and pray change if you entered into and submitted to this reality?

Does the track record of the church's disunity prove Jesus' prayer a failure? Why or why not?

Have you ever been on one side or the other of a church or denominational split? How was Jesus' prayer for unity talked about, ignored, or dismissed as irrelevant?

Does your church emphasize unity or diversity? What problems occur by emphasizing one or the other instead of both?

Praying with Jesus

Father, make us one — with you, the Trinity, and with other Christians. Help us see this unity so that we are not tempted to try to make a false unity ourselves. Amen.

Jesus Prays the Agony of Gethsemane:
Matthew 26:39, 42

(pp. 231-38)

Summary

The Christian life follows Jesus to the cross, where he freely accepts his death in obedience to his Father. But Jesus doesn't just go to the cross; he *prays* his way to the cross.

There is a consistency to Jesus' prayers, even in the face of death. His Gethsemane praying echoes the Lord's Prayer. And even though his prayer partners abandon him, falling asleep on him and then deserting him, he is prepared for what comes next because his prayers have developed obedience in him.

Quotes for Consideration

"The cup is a container from which we take something that is not us into our lives so that it becomes us, entering into our living." (p. 231)

"In a religious atmosphere that was stagnant with the bad breath of nit-picking moralism, Jesus was a fresh breeze." (p. 232)

"[Jesus' prayers] are a strong defense against the persistent satanic illusions that seduce us with promises that if only we follow Jesus' life we will be trouble free, pain free, boredom free, anxiety free." (p. 233)

"Prayer accomplishes within us, within our spirits, deep within our souls, what is later lived out in the circumstances and conditions of our obedience." (p. 237)

63

"Prayer goes beneath the surface and penetrates to the heart of the matter. Unlike mere action, prayer is not subject to immediate evaluation or verification." (p. 237)

"If we are addicted to 'results' we will quickly lose interest in prayer. When we pray we willingly participate in what God is doing, without knowing precisely what God is doing, how God is doing it, or when we will know what is going on — if ever." (p. 237)

"Action without prayer thins out into something merely exterior." (p. 238)

"A prayerless life can result in effective action and accomplish magnificent things, but if there is no developed interiority, the action never enters into the depth and intricacy of relationships where the stuff of creation is formed, where salvation is worked, where men and women find themselves present and at home with the ways of God." (p. 238)

Questions for Interaction

Which do you believe is more effective: doing something or praying? Which do you do more of? How might you shift from relying on acting over praying to praying over acting?

Peterson writes, "If we are addicted to 'results' we will quickly lose interest in prayer" (p. 237). When have you given up praying for someone or something because you didn't get the results you wanted? Did God come through in some shape or form later on anyway?

How prayerful are your actions recently? How might you keep your actions prayerful?

How interior or exterior is your faith? Are you prayerfully deep and actively wide?

Praying with Jesus

My Father, if it is possible, let this cup pass from me; yet not what I want but what you want. My Father, if this cannot pass unless I drink it, your will be done.

Jesus Prays from the Cross: The Seven Last Words

(pp. 239-60)

Summary

Jesus prayed seven one-sentence prayers from the cross that are tied to each other even though they are spread out over the four Gospels.

Jesus' death was a real, historical death. And it is a great mystery: that Life could die; that his death could bring us life. But not only that, his death becomes a pattern for our lives. We live by dying with him. Choosing to follow him is suicide, a self-denying self-death.

My God, my God, why have you forsaken me? There is no avoiding death. And far from avoiding it, we plunge into it metaphorically as we follow Jesus, dying daily. And as he and we experience it, we cry out, "Why?" But the psalm from which Jesus' dying "Why?" came (Psalm 22) ends differently than it begins, moving from a sense of abandonment to being surrounded by God's people. Even in the aloneness of death, the company of the resurrected are implied. So, even feeling abandoned, Jesus and we keep praying.

Father, forgive them; for they know not what they do. While dying, Jesus forgives those who participated in killing him: Judas, Jews, Pilate, soldiers, disciples. They were all guilty. But he absolves them, forgives. Justice is important, but it isn't the last word. Forgiveness is. As we pray this prayer, we move from revenge to compassion.

Truly I tell you, today you will be with me in Paradise. There is something beyond this life. It doesn't just end with the grave. Unfortunately, we've turned heaven and hell speculation into projections of eternal self-indulgence and childish fantasy. Jesus simply says, "With me. Today." What more do we need to know?

Father, into your hands I commend my spirit. In childlike trust, Jesus offers his spirit to his Father. This child-prayer is in stark contrast to the horrific setting in which it was prayed. There are times to be asked to be delivered from evil and times to deliver our spirits to God in the face of evil. We need both prayers at our disposal, both on a daily basis.

Woman, here is your son. . . . Here is your mother. Jesus doesn't neglect the domestic for the spiritual. Real people. Real relationships. These are why Jesus went to the cross, and he wasn't going to turn his back on them while on the cross. This is "prayed" love for the ones in front of our faces.

I thirst. Jesus wasn't just a spiritual presence. He suffered in his body and died. He can never be separated from his body, which grew thirsty as he died.

It is finished. Just as God declared creation complete, Jesus declares salvation complete. No petering out. Jesus has accomplished what he set out to do. No loose ends. Any attempt to add to what Jesus has done is to be rejected.

Quotes for Consideration

"Death is the defining act ('reason') of Jesus' life." (p. 239)
"Each prayer stands on its own, but none is in isolation from the others."
    (p. 239)
"Christians die twice. The first death is when we set out to follow Jesus. . . . We pray in company with Jesus as he prays his death. As we
    do this, our death gets included in his death." (p. 241)
"Meditating and praying with Jesus as he dies on the cross is not an invitation to morbidity. . . . We begin all our prayers, and most emphatically these prayers from the cross, at the empty tomb, the place of
    resurrection." (p. 242)
"Cross and resurrection are the south and north poles, true gospel polarities, of a single, undivided, salvation world. Remove either pole and
    you gut salvation." (p. 243)
"Faith in God is not an escape from reality. Faith in God is a plunge into

reality in all its dimensions, and not the least of these realities is death." (p. 244)

"The act of forgiveness does not eliminate concerns for justice, but it does introduce a personal dimension into those concerns that give witness to the gospel." (p. 247)

"However important justice is — and it *is* important — forgiveness is more important." (p. 248)

"Forgiveness is not soft sentimentality. It is hard-edged gospel." (p. 248)

"I find it significant that it is a crucified criminal who is the first to recognize that Jesus on the cross is his savior and, with no moral or righteous qualifications, is saved." (p. 250)

"It is essential that we not let our emotional or physical circumstances dictate the language of our prayers." (p. 252)

"The reality of our bodies in our daily dying must also be included in our prayers — and not just as an afterthought." (p. 257)

"Spiritual pornography is prayer and faith without relationship, intimacy with Jesus reduced and debased into an idea or cause to be argued and used." (p. 257)

"We are set free for the act of obedient faith, the one human action in which we don't get *in* the way but are *on* the way." (p. 260)

Questions for Interaction

Following Jesus requires death on our part. Where are you holding back on taking up your cross, on choosing to follow Jesus in death for the sake of others?

How does it change your praying to join Jesus as he prays, "My God, my God, why have you forsaken me?" How does it change your praying to know that he prays with you in your forsakenness?

What injustice are you struggling to forgive? Which is easier: to seek justice or to offer forgiveness? Why?

How does Jesus' response ("with me," "today") to the thief on the cross shape your view of death and beyond?

In the midst of mockery and deadly pain, Jesus trustingly laid his spirit into the Father's hands. When have you been able to prayerfully do the same?

A childlike trust in good times is easy. How does Jesus' prayerful companionship enable you to trust our Father in deep adversity?

When do we ask to be delivered from evil and when do we commit our spirits to our Father?

Other cultures obsess about death. What is wrong with that? Why do we hide death like an embarrassment? How do the prayers of Jesus from the cross keep us immersed in both death *and* life (resurrection)?

Even in the midst of winning our salvation, Jesus doesn't neglect down-to-earth domestic and family relations. How can over-spiritualization weaken our praying? How can everyday loving of others in prayer deepen our praying, especially during suffering?

How does the sheer physicalness of Jesus' suffering and praying shape your physical suffering and praying?

Only one of Jesus' seven words/prayers from the cross came out of physical suffering. How does this validate and encourage our prayers for physical concerns? How does this limit prayers for health and physical concerns? What percentage of your prayers deal with physical issues (meals, health, etc.)? Are they in good proportion to the rest of who you are?

How does the prayed completion of Jesus' work of salvation free up our prayers? Free us up to participate in his work without having to take over and make it happen?

Praying with Jesus

Forsaken One, you continued to pray, even as you experienced forsakenness by the Father. Pray with me as I take up my cross and follow you, that I may not stop praying either. Amen.

SESSION 20

Praying in Jesus' Name: Acorns into Oak Trees

(pp. 261-70)

Summary

Christians pray "in the name" of Jesus. We pray in a world shaped by Jesus. We pray in the way of Jesus and by the authority of Jesus.

How we use words matters. Just like in the Garden, sin and evil, more often than not, begin with a misuse of language. Words can be used to cover and hide instead of to reveal and open up in intimacy.

Listening to and praying with the prayers of Jesus pulls us out of ourselves when we pray while giving a good but unself-conscious shape to our prayers. As we pray the Lord's Prayer and other repeated prayers, we learn to pray in ways that aren't determined by our feelings and circumstances but by the kingdom of God. And when we pray spontaneously, having been schooled by Jesus in his prayers, we bring our feelings and circumstances to God in a personal, relational way.

Prayer isn't us gathering up our spiritual energies so we can do something in the world. Rather, it is mostly the Holy Spirit doing something in us, making God known and bringing out the responses of praise, petition, and obedience.

Prayer bridges the divide we create between the sacred and the secular, connecting God and the daily. And while our individual prayers are engaged in personally, praying in Jesus' name keeps us from privatizing prayer, keeping us connected with the communion of the saints.

Not everything we say is prayer. But all our words and silences can be. Praying without ceasing is "our entire lives gathered in intention before God, leaving nothing and no one out" (p. 268). It infuses the secular with the holy. It looks for Jesus everywhere, listening for his speaking and praying and joining with him in it.

The veil of the Holy of Holies protected spirituality from becoming a manipulation of God. It trained people to be aware of the holy. When the veil was torn, the Holy Place became Every Place, heaven was married to earth. No walls.

Jesus' prayers, planted in the soil of our souls, grow up in us, and become an oak tree of prayer rooted in the common, day-to-day affairs of the earth and reaching into heaven.

Quotes for Consideration

"The general mess in which we now find ourselves originates in a misuse of language." (p. 263)

"Fig-leaf language deals with God but in a way that subtly avoids God." (p. 264)

"Language is sacred. All words are holy. But when they are torn out of the story that God speaks into being and then used apart from God, language is desecrated: words become non-personal, words become non-relational." (p. 264)

"We learn the language of prayer by immersing ourselves in the language that God uses to reveal himself to us, the Jesus-language world. . . . Our prayers are no longer shaped by our culture. . . . Our prayers are rescued from being conditioned by our psyche." (p. 266)

"God listens to us; we listen to God. God speaks to us; we speak to God. It would be too much to say that it is a conversation between equals, but at least both parties are speaking the same language, a language of revelation, a deeply relational language, not an informational language, not a manipulative language." (p. 266)

"Prayer is not gathering up our spiritual energies to make a statement or launch a cause." (p. 266)

"Prayer is alert to tendencies within ourselves that privatize prayer and insulate us from the company of the communion of saints." (p. 267)

"Prayer is a way of language practiced in the presence of God in which we become more than ourselves while remaining ourselves." (p. 267)

"I want to knock down the fences that keep prayer confined to religious

settings and religious subjects. . . . I want to participate in prayers that don't sound like prayers. Prayers that in the praying aren't identified as prayers. Prayers without ceasing." (p. 268)

"A people of God are always in need of thoroughgoing training in holiness." (p. 269)

"All language is available for giving witness to the holy, to name the holy, wherever and whenever, just as Jesus used and uses language." (p. 270)

"Jesus' prayers do not contain all prayer. They are acorns from which a praying life grows in us, becoming deep-rooted, heaven-reaching oak trees." (p. 270)

Questions for Interaction

How have you prayed to God and yet hid from God by the words you used and/or didn't use?

In what ways do you and others pray and yet avoid dealing with God?

How do misused, desecrated words end up misusing and desecrating God, people, creation?

Why are spontaneous prayers, rising from our hearts and circumstances, so important?

Why are repeated prayers, which take us beyond our feelings and circumstances, so important?

Is it possible that you pray more often and in more ways than you are aware of? How might all your speaking be done in the presence of God, with a knowledge of his active listening, turning it all into prayer?

The veil of the Holy of Holies protected spirituality from becoming a manipulation of God. What are the benefits brought by the removal of the veil? What are the liabilities that ease of access to God in prayer has brought?

Praying with Jesus

Jesus, it is in your name that I live and pray. Not by my strength. Not to my glory. I want to participate in your praying. I want to leave no one and nothing out of the scope of my praying so that I will know what it means to pray without ceasing. Amen.

www.ingramcontent.com/pod-product-compliance
Lightning Source LLC
Chambersburg PA
CBHW031004090426
42737CB00008B/674